8-26-19

WHEREVER YOU GO, GO WITH ALL YOUR HEART

Compiled by
Hannah Beilenson

PETER PAUPER PRESS, INC.
White Plains, New York

FOR MY MOTHER—ALWAYS MINDFUL,
ALWAYS READY FOR THE NEXT ADVENTURE.

Designed by Margaret Rubiano

Illustrations used under license
from Shutterstock.com

Copyright © 2019
Peter Pauper Press, Inc.
202 Mamaroneck Avenue
White Plains, NY 10601 USA
All rights reserved
ISBN 978-1-4413-2919-6
Printed in China

7 6 5 4 3 2 1

Visit us at www.peterpauper.com

WHEREVER you GO, GO WITH ALL YOUR HEART

WHEREVER YOU GO, GO WITH ALL YOUR HEART

The aim of life is to live, and to live means to be aware, joyously, drunkenly, serenely, divinely aware.

—HENRY MILLER

What does it take to make a journey? Not a car or a plane ticket, those things only start you on your way. A sense of wonder, mindfulness, and awareness of the world around you—these are what make an adventure meaningful. Do you experience each moment to its full potential? Do you believe it's not just about where you are, but how you are? Do you ever find yourself taking notice of something small—the grass cracking out of concrete, the clouds gray and thin like steam over hot bread—and realize that beauty can only be recognized when you're awake to it? If so, may this volume speak to you. Filled with quotes from figures of all times, places, and walks of life, this book revels in the little wonders that exist everywhere, and is small enough to keep close wherever your travels take you.

BE PRESENT IN ALL
THAT ONE DOES, FROM
THE EFFORT OF
LOVING TO THE
BREAKING OF BREAD.

JAMES BALDWIN

Come forth into
the light of things,
let Nature be
your Teacher.

WILLIAM WORDSWORTH

The universe is full of magical things patiently waiting for our wits to grow sharper.

EDEN PHILLPOTTS

TOMORROW IS TOMORROW. FUTURE CARES HAVE FUTURE CURES, AND WE MUST MIND TODAY.

SOPHOCLES

It's wonderful to climb the liquid mountains of the sky. Behind me and before me is God and I have no fears.

HELEN KELLER

ADVENTURE MUST BE
HELD IN DELICATE
FINGERS. IT SHOULD
BE HANDLED, NOT
EMBRACED. IT SHOULD
BE SIPPED, NOT
SWALLOWED AT A GULP.

ASHLEY DUKES

A moment's insight
is sometimes worth
a life's experience.

OLIVER WENDELL HOLMES, SR.

As surely as
there is a voyage
away, there is a
journey home.

JACK KORNFIELD

I MEAN TO ELIMINATE
ALL WASTE, DEADNESS,
SUPERFLUITY:
TO GIVE THE MOMENT
WHOLE; WHATEVER
IT INCLUDES.

VIRGINIA WOOLF

Almost anything
will work again
if you unplug it
for a few minutes,
including you.

ANNE LAMOTT

You don't take a photograph, you make it.

ANSEL ADAMS

WHENEVER YOU ARE ABLE TO
OBSERVE YOUR MIND, YOU ARE
NO LONGER TRAPPED IN IT.

ECKHART TOLLE

*Stop a moment,
cease your work, look
around you.*

LEO TOLSTOY

For always roaming
with a hungry
heart, much have I
seen and known.

ALFRED TENNYSON

THE CLEAREST WAY
INTO THE UNIVERSE
IS THROUGH A
FOREST WILDERNESS.

JOHN MUIR

THE REAL MEANING
OF TRAVEL, LIKE
THAT OF A CONVERSATION
BY THE FIRESIDE, IS THE
DISCOVERY OF ONESELF
THROUGH CONTACT WITH
OTHER PEOPLE.

PAUL TOURNIER

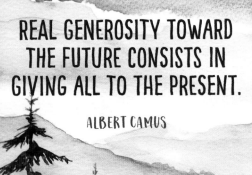

REAL GENEROSITY TOWARD
THE FUTURE CONSISTS IN
GIVING ALL TO THE PRESENT.

ALBERT CAMUS

To pay attention,
this is our endless
and proper work.

MARY OLIVER

BE HERE NOW.

RAM DASS

You cannot control the results, only your actions.

ALLAN LOKOS

DON'T TRY TO UNDERSTAND LIFE. LIVE IT!

OSHO

BE HAPPY IN THE MOMENT, THAT'S ENOUGH. EACH MOMENT IS ALL WE NEED, NOT MORE.

MOTHER TERESA

LIVING IN THE MOMENT
MEANS LETTING GO OF
THE PAST AND NOT
WAITING FOR THE FUTURE.
IT MEANS LIVING YOUR
LIFE CONSCIOUSLY, AWARE
THAT EACH MOMENT YOU
BREATHE IS A GIFT.

OPRAH WINFREY

There are many, many details of action involved in the simplicity and sharpness of being in this very moment, here, now.

CHÖGYAM TRUNGPA

MINDFULNESS TRAINS US TO BE AWAKE AND ALIVE, FULLY CURIOUS, ABOUT NOW.

PEMA CHÖDRÖN

We're so busy watching out for what's just ahead of us that we don't take the time to enjoy where we are.

BILL WATTERSON

STUFF YOUR EYES
WITH WONDER.... SEE
THE WORLD. IT'S MORE
FANTASTIC THAN ANY
DREAM MADE OR PAID
FOR IN FACTORIES.

RAY BRADBURY

He who wonders
discovers that
this is in itself
a wonder.

M. C. ESCHER

WE CARRY WITHIN US
THE WONDERS WE SEEK
WITHOUT US.

THOMAS BROWNE

The secret of
seeing is to sail on
a solar wind.

ANNIE DILLARD

TO SEE CLEARLY IS POETRY, PROPHECY, AND RELIGION— ALL IN ONE.

JOHN RUSKIN

SOME OF THE
GREATEST POETRY IS
REVEALING TO THE
READER THE BEAUTY
IN SOMETHING SO
SIMPLE YOU HAD
TAKEN IT FOR GRANTED.

NEIL DEGRASSE TYSON

We don't see things as they are, we see them as we are.

ANAÏS NIN

OUR SOCIETY IS MUCH MORE
INTERESTED IN INFORMATION
THAN WONDER, IN NOISE
RATHER THAN SILENCE.... WE
NEED A LOT MORE WONDER
AND A LOT MORE SILENCE
IN OUR LIVES.

MR. ROGERS

Let go of your
mind and then
be mindful.
Close your ears
and listen!

RUMI

ONE DOESN'T DISCOVER
NEW LANDS WITHOUT
CONSENTING TO LOSE
SIGHT, FOR A VERY LONG
TIME, OF THE SHORE.

ANDRE GIDE

THE RIVER IS CONSTANTLY
TURNING AND BENDING
AND YOU NEVER KNOW
WHERE IT'S GOING TO GO
AND WHERE YOU'LL WIND UP.
FOLLOWING... IT... MEANS
THAT YOU ARE ON THE
RIGHT TRACK.

EARTHA KITT

No amount of regretting can change the past, and no amount of worrying can change the future.

ROY T. BENNETT

A MAN TRAVELS
THE WORLD OVER IN
SEARCH OF WHAT HE
NEEDS AND RETURNS
HOME TO FIND IT.

GEORGE MOORE

Traveling is not just seeing the new; it is also leaving behind. Not just opening doors; also closing them behind you, never to return.

JAN MYRDAL

LIKE A FISH BREAKING
A NET IN THE WATER,
NOT RETURNING, LIKE A
FIRE NOT GOING BACK
TO WHAT IS ALREADY
BURNED, ONE SHOULD
WANDER SOLITARY AS
A RHINOCEROS HORN.

BUDDHA

TO SEE A WORLD IN A GRAIN
OF SAND, AND A HEAVEN IN A
WILD FLOWER, HOLD INFINITY
IN THE PALM OF YOUR HAND,
AND ETERNITY IN AN HOUR.

WILLIAM BLAKE

Listen to yourself, and in that quietude you might hear the voice of God.

MAYA ANGELOU

I KNOW NOT ALL THAT
MAY BE COMING, BUT BE
IT WHAT IT WILL, I'LL GO
TO IT LAUGHING.

HERMAN MELVILLE

Feelings come and go like clouds in a windy sky. Conscious breathing is my anchor.

THICH NHAT HANH

YOU MUST LIVE IN THE PRESENT, LAUNCH YOURSELF ON EVERY WAVE, FIND YOUR ETERNITY IN EACH MOMENT.

HENRY DAVID THOREAU

MEDITATION IS THE ULTIMATE MOBILE DEVICE; YOU CAN USE IT ANYWHERE, ANYTIME, UNOBTRUSIVELY.

SHARON SALZBERG

When the path
reveals itself,
follow it.

CHERYL STRAYED

Stop trying to be who you think you should be — become who you are.

RASHEED OGUNLARU

THE PURPOSE OF LIFE
IS TO LIVE IT, TO TASTE
EXPERIENCE TO THE
UTMOST, TO REACH OUT
EAGERLY AND WITHOUT
FEAR FOR NEWER
AND RICHER EXPERIENCE.

ELEANOR ROOSEVELT

IF WE ARE HOLDING BACK
FROM ANY PART OF OUR
EXPERIENCE ... WE ARE
FUELING THE FEARS AND
FEELINGS OF SEPARATION
THAT SUSTAIN THE TRANCE
OF UNWORTHINESS.

TARA BRACH

If you want to conquer the anxiety of life, live in the moment, live in the breath.

AMIT RAY

HISTORY IS MORE OR LESS BUNK. IT'S TRADITION. WE DON'T WANT TRADITION. WE WANT TO LIVE IN THE PRESENT.

HENRY FORD

Let's not look back in anger, or forward in fear, but around in awareness.

JAMES THURBER

THE WATER YOU TOUCH IN A RIVER IS THE LAST OF THAT WHICH HAS PASSED, AND THE FIRST OF THAT WHICH IS COMING. THUS IT IS WITH TIME PRESENT.

LEONARDO DA VINCI

We're always getting ready to live, but never living.

RALPH WALDO EMERSON

THE ONLY THING
THAT CAN SAVE
THE WORLD IS THE
RECLAIMING OF
THE AWARENESS
OF THE WORLD.

ALLEN GINSBERG

Never lose the child-like wonder. It's just too important. It's what drives us.

RANDY PAUSCH

Life is what
happens to us while
we are making
other plans.

ALLEN SAUNDERS

EVERY TIME WE BECOME
AWARE OF A THOUGHT, AS
OPPOSED TO BEING LOST IN
A THOUGHT, WE EXPERIENCE
THAT OPENING OF THE MIND.

JOSEPH GOLDSTEIN

The more I wonder
the more I love.

ALICE WALKER

WHAT KEEPS YOU
GOING ISN'T SOME FINE
DESTINATION BUT JUST
THE ROAD YOU'RE ON,
AND THE FACT THAT YOU
KNOW HOW TO DRIVE.

BARBARA KINGSOLVER

The world will
never starve for
want of wonders;
but only for want
of wonder.

G. K. CHESTERTON